PIANO
Adventures by Nancy and Randall Faber
Jazz & Blues

ies

6

This book belongs to: _____

Arranged by

Nancy and Randall Faber

Production Coordinator: Jon Ophoff
Design and Illustration: Terpstra Design, San Francisco
Engraving: Dovetree Productions, Inc.

FABER
PIANO ADVENTURES®
3042 Creek Drive
Ann Arbor, Michigan 48108

A NOTE TO TEACHERS

The **Piano Adventures® Student Choice Series** offers an exciting set of arrangements in a variety of genres and at just the right level of difficulty.

This selection of **Level 6** pieces is designed to be fun, showy, and to inspire enthusiasm and pride in the intermediate piano student.

Invite your student to choose from additional styles in the series, each arranged at six levels, including:

- Popular
- Classics
- Jazz & Blues
- Christmas
- Studio Collection

Visit **www.PianoAdventures.com**

De **Piano Adventures® Student Choice Series** bevat fascinerende arrangementen in een keur aan stijlen, precies op het juiste niveau.

Met deze selectie van stukken in **niveau 6** kan de half gevorderde leerling zich met trots presenteren. Het is vooral plezierig, inspirerend en enthousiasmerend repertoire.

Er zijn arrangementen op 6 verschillende niveaus. Uw leerling kan kiezen uit vele stijlen, waaronder:

- Popular
- Classics
- Jazz & Blues
- Christmas
- Studio Collection

Bezoek ons op **www.PianoAdventures.nl**

La serie dei volumi **Student Choice** di **Piano Adventures®** offre una straordinaria gamma di arrangiamenti di diversi generi musicali e livelli di difficoltà.

La selezione del **Livello 6** è concepita per essere divertente e di grande impatto e per ispirare entusiasmo nell'allievo di livello intermedio.

Invita i tuoi studenti a scegliere tra gli altri stili proposti dalla serie, ognuno dei quali è arrangiato a sei livelli di difficoltà e comprende:

- Pop
- Classici
- Jazz & Blues
- Natale
- Studio Collection

Visita **www.PianoAdventures.it**

Die Hefte der Reihe **Student Choice Series** von **Piano Adventures®** bieten anregende Arrangements im passenden Schwierigkeitsgrad und in unterschiedlichen Stilrichtungen.

Stufe 6: Mit dieser Auswahl an Stücken kann sich der nun leicht fortgeschrittene Schüler mit Stolz und Bravour präsentieren. Dies inspiriert und macht Spaß zugleich.

Lassen Sie Ihre Schüler aus den folgenden jeweils in sechs Stufen vorliegenden Heften wählen:

- Popular
- Classics
- Jazz & Blues
- Christmas
- Studio Collection

Besuchen Sie uns: **www.PianoAdventures.de**

La **serie de libros suplementarios "Student Choice"** de **Piano Adventures®** ofrece adaptaciones de piezas cautivadoras en una gran variedad de géneros y niveles de dificultad.

Las piezas divertidas y llamativas del **Nivel 6** despiertan el entusiasmo y el orgullo de los estudiantes de nivel intermedio temprano.

Invite a sus estudiantes a elegir entre los siguientes estilos, cada uno disponible en seis niveles:

- Popular
- Clásicos
- *Jazz* y *Blues*
- Navidad
- *Studio Collection*

Para más información, visite **www.PianoAdventures-es.com**

TABLE OF CONTENTS

IEFF1011

Take the "A" Train

Words and Music by
BILLY STRAYHORN

6

7

Autumn Leaves

English lyrics by JOHNNY MERCER
French lyrics by JACQUES PREVERT

Music by
JOSEPH KOSMA

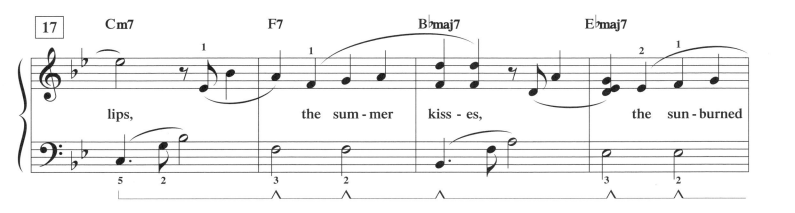

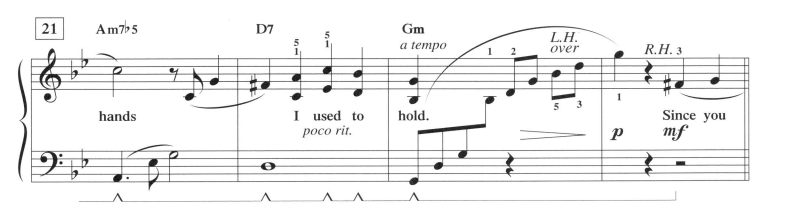

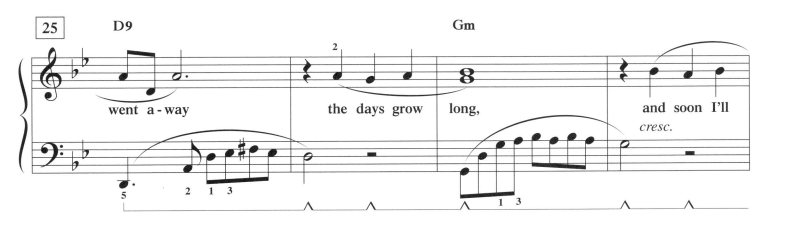

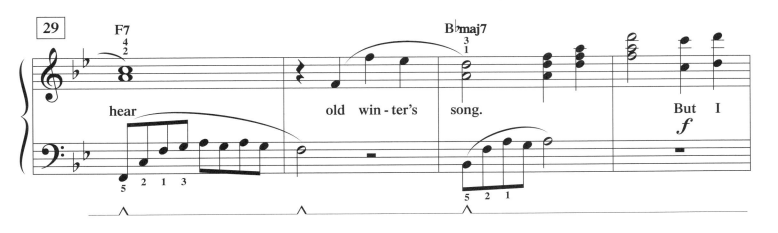

Georgia on My Mind

Lyrics by
STUART GORRELL

Music by
HOAGY CARMICHAEL

IEFF1011

12

Satin Doll

Words by
JOHNNY MERCER
and BILLY STRAYHORN

Music by
DUKE ELLINGTON

15

IEFF1011

Big City Blues

NANCY FABER

Cast Your Fate to the Wind

Lyrics by CAREL WERBER
Music by VINCE GUARALDI

Misty

Words by
JOHNNY BURKE

Music by
ERROLL GARNER

Locomotive Blues

Moving steadily, no swing

RANDALL FABER

Lullaby of Birdland

Words by GEORGE DAVID WEISS
Music by GEORGE SHEARING

Perdido

ERVIN DRAKE, HARRY LENK,
and JUAN TIZOL

Desafinado

Original lyrics by NEWTON MENDONCA
Music by ANTONIO CARLOS JOBIM

Bossa nova tempo (no swing)

Night Train

**JIMMY FORREST,
OSCAR WASHINGTON,
and LEWIS C. SIMPKINS**

IEFF1011

Equinox

NANCY FABER

All the Things You Are

**Lyrics by
OSCAR HAMMERSTEIN II**

**Music by
JEROME KERN**

IEFF1011

A Taste of Honey

Words by
RIC MARLOW

Music by
BOBBY SCOTT